RACING FOR THE PEOPLE

Christiana Cobb-Dozier
Illustrated by: Kimiyo

Racing For The People

Copyright © 2020 by Christiana Cobb-Dozier

First Edition

Hardcover ISBN: 978-1-64990-807-0
Paperback ISBN: 978-1-64990-814-8
eBook ISBN: 978-1-64990-559-8

Dedicated to Tommie Smith, John Carlos
and freedom fighters everywhere.

Fists of honor,

Fists of glory

This is their story.

Two boys who became men

Making history with their victories

Fighting to the finish.

Called unworthy by the color of their skin,

They became an inspiration.

Their stories did not start on the track,

They had to prove their strength.

Their bravery and pride shocked the world

With more than just a race.

"Pop!"

The gun sounded for the start of the race.
Eight runners sped around the track,
arms swinging and legs pumping.

"Hurray!"

The crowd cheered as John Carlos took a brief lead with Tommie Smith on his heels. John couldn't believe it. He glanced at Tommie for a moment before Tommie zoomed past him and took first place.

Victory!

Tommie crossed the finish line and won the race
with Australian runner
Peter Norman in second, and John in third.

The crowd watched as they took the stage for their medals. As the runners approached the medal stand, Tommie and John's eyes were serious.

Heads down, fists up. Their silence and their fists meant power and pride for their people.

"Boo! Stop! Get out of here!"

The crowd became angry at Tommie and John as they raised their fists high, but the two did not budge. They became heroes for Black, poor and hurting people in America on October 16, 1968. But before that moment, they were young boys with hopes and dreams that led them to the medal stand.

Before John was blazing the track, he was a little boy running around the streets of Harlem, New York in the 1950s. It was the Harlem Renaissance, a time when jazz and blues music filled the air. The summers were hot and the pools were warm. He loved laughing with his friends as they swam and played, but life wasn't all fun and games.

Walking around his neighborhood, John would see his neighbors and friends sick. Drugs and violence were all over Harlem. John was happy at home, but his friends had nights filled with crying and yelling.

"I don't know my dad," one friend told John. His friend told him that his mom took care of him, his brothers and sisters all on her own. "I have a big family, and sometimes it's hard for my mom, so she cries when we don't have a lot of food for dinner," he told him.

"It's not fair that my friends can't have what I have," John thought to himself. "What if my friends had someone to help them so they were never hungry?"

John decided to help his friends. He felt fortunate to have both of his parents at home with him, working very hard so he could have everything he needed. "No one should have to be hungry or feel like they are less important than anyone else," John thought.

So one day as John watched Robin Hood, he wondered, "Hmm, my friends need help, and some people have more than enough. I'll just take it!"
John wanted to be Robin Hood for his neighborhood.

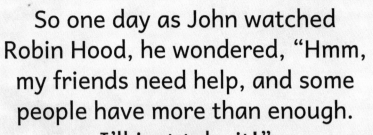

"I know! I'll take from the rich and give to the poor, just like Robin Hood. Robin Hood was a hero because he helped people who really needed it. I'll be a hero too and my friends won't have to worry anymore."

Dodging the police daily, John raced through his neighborhood to see his friends happy. He knew he was breaking the law, but he cared more that he was helping others.

Across the country, on a farm in Lemoore, California, lived Tommie Smith. The sun would beat down on Tommie and his 11 brothers and sisters as they spent hours working in the fields picking cotton, grapes and strawberries. Summers were hot and sometimes unbearable, but working in the fields was one of the only ways that young Black children could make money.

As a boy, Tommie suffered
from pneumonia and it was hard
for him to breathe most days.
But pneumonia didn't stop Tommie.

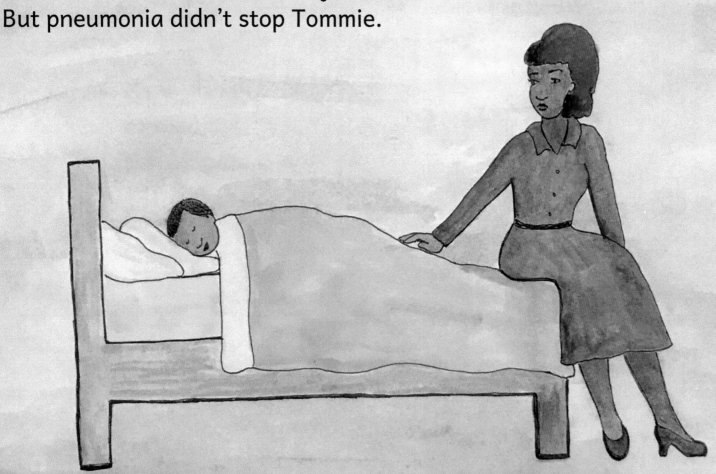

Something inside of him pushed him to never give up.
He grew healthier each day, fighting the pneumonia
until he won.

By the time Tommie was in high school,
he was regularly winning in foot races
with his classmates. Basketball, football,
track and field, it didn't matter; Tommie
aimed for excellence, breaking records and
becoming MVP in all three sports.

The track stars met at San Jose State University in "Speed City" San Jose, California; known for its top-notch track team, running laps around the competition.

Tommie went to San Jose State to be a basketball star, but track coach Bud Winters won him over. His quick feet and athleticism made him perfect for the track.

Off the track, the hard reality was that it was
the 1960s and segregation, separating white people
from people of color, was normal at the time.

Just like Harlem and other cities around the country,
Black people were hungry, sick or living in run-down homes
because of the color of their skin. This sadness
raised up activists and community leaders
like Malcolm X, whom John looked up to for lessons
of pride in himself as a Black man.

Harry Edwards, an activist and former San Jose State discus thrower, taught and mentored Tommie to be a strong athlete and activist. He encouraged him to always speak out for change in the community.

"Being an athlete is more important than winning the race," Harry lectured the runners.

"You have a responsibility to our people. It is time to train for the Olympic Human Rights Project."

Tommie was set to race for the people in the 1968 Olympics
with a protest for the world to see. It wasn't long before John
joined the team and sparked a fire for the movement.
He was feisty and fast. His quick mouth matched with his athletic
ability made him the right addition to the team. The many lessons
he learned from Malcolm X on the streets of Harlem,
prepared him for this moment.

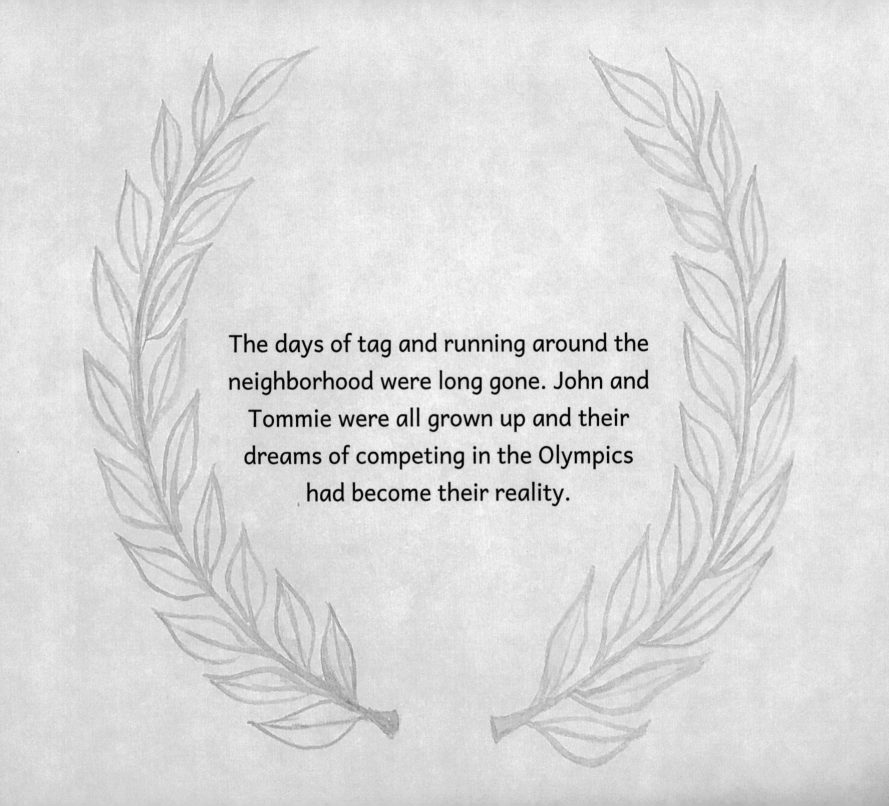

The days of tag and running around the neighborhood were long gone. John and Tommie were all grown up and their dreams of competing in the Olympics had become their reality.

October 16, 1968, Mexico City.

This day changed their lives forever. The racers planned
to make a powerful statement at the end of the race,
so they had to win, not just for the medals
but for the people. They needed to win for justice.

On your mark, get set, go!

The racers took off! Tommie pushed hard and was quickly
in first place! John was shocked. Tommie in first,
Peter Norman in second, and he in third.

The race was over and it was time to make a statement. Tommie and John walked up to the medal stand, took off their shoes and stepped onto the podiums revealing their black socks which symbolized the many poor families around America. John took a deep breath and remembered all his friends in Harlem who didn't have food.

He stood for them.

"USA, USA,"

The crowd shouted as they raised their black-gloved fists.
Tommie's right fist symbolized power and human rights
and John's left fist was raised for unity. They bowed
their heads in prayer and reflection as silence fell and the crowd
became angry. The crowd could not believe
Tommie and John's boldness.

Tommie and John risked their Olympic medals
and their physical safety to send a message of pride,
love and peace, but people yelled and called them
hurtful names. The crowd was so angry, they could
not see that Tommie and John were using their bodies
and wearing different symbols to send a message
for justice.

They wore beaded necklaces for the history of lynching;
in memory of the many Black people who died from hangings
because of slavery, segregation, and racism. Tommie also
wore a black scarf for Black pride and held an olive branch
for peace. Their actions were subtle but had much power.
John unzipped his tracksuit for the hard-working families
around the country. And finally, uniting them together,
were their badges for the Olympics for
Human Rights Project. They raced for the people.

Despite the anger and misunderstanding from the crowd,
their message was worldwide and timeless.
They stood for change and today many are
still standing and fighting. Tommie and John
stood with their fists in the air for the innocent people
hurting and dying because of racism and injustice.

From running around neighborhood streets,

As kids with little cares

To running for change in the in the 1968 Olympic race,

For good and against despair.

The crowd judged and anger brewed,

They risked everything that day.

But the message was greater than any risk,

So they lifted their fists and prayed.

So when it is you with an injustice to face

What will be your response?

Will you sit and let wrong happen or will you stand and fight?

Like Tommie and John,

Will you stand up for what is right?

Glossary:

Activist: Someone who works for social or political change.

Lynching: A form of killing someone by hanging from a tree; popular during the Jim Crow era.

Oppression: Cruel or unjust treatment or control for a long time.

Protest: A form of expressing disagreement with something politically or socially.

Racism: Anger, judgement, criticism or violence directed at someone because of their race with the belief that one's own race is superior to another.

Segregation: Separation of people, seen during the 1900s with Jim Crow laws separating white people from people of color, specifically Black people.

About the Author

Christiana is a queer African American school counselor who is dedicated to her students, walking with them as they journey toward the best versions of themselves. Originally from Sacramento, California, her educational endeavors took her to San Jose State University where she earned her BS in journalism, and the University of Southern California where she earned her M.E.D. in school counseling.

Writing has always been a passion of Christiana's. As an undergraduate, she was inspired by the stories of Olympic runners Tommie Smith and John Carlos, who often visited her university and motivated students to be active in making change for their communities. She recognized their stories as an unsung piece of the civil rights movement that not enough children grow up hearing.

One summer she volunteered to read at a reading enrichment program for African American youth, and wanted to read a story about these Olympic heroes for the children. But there were none, so she decided to write it herself. It is Christiana's desire is to add to the vast collection of civil rights non-fiction children's stories.

About the Illustrator

Kimiyo, as a coach, counselor and artist, hopes to promote equity and justice to inspire all ages to pursue their dreams. She grew up in Dallas, TX, and pursued higher education at the University of Southern California receiving her BA in Theater and a M.Ed in school counseling. Kimiyo currently lives in Bellingham, WA with her husband and two dogs where she finds joy in dancing, acting and of course, drawing!

CPSIA information can be obtained at www.ICGtesting.com
Printed in the USA
LVIW011020050221
678464LV00019B/187